JOKES FOR Kids

"**Introducing Angelo White**, the author of the highly-anticipated book "Jokes for Kids: A Guide to Creating Hilarious Jokes." Angelo is a master of comedy and in this book, he shares his expertise on how to create jokes that will have kids laughing out loud. He draws from his own experience as a comedian and a father to offer tips, tricks, and techniques for crafting jokes that are both funny and appropriate for children.

In "Jokes for Kids," Angelo covers a wide range of topics, from puns and wordplay to silly situations and characters. He also includes interactive exercises and prompts to help readers come up with their own jokes. This book is not only a great way to entertain kids, but it also helps to encourage reading, learning new words, and improving vocabulary, creativity, and imagination.

Whether you're a parent, a teacher, or simply looking for a fun way to engage with kids, "Jokes for Kids" is the perfect guide. With Angelo's clever humor and his wealth of experience, you'll be crafting jokes that will have kids (and adults) laughing in no time. Get your copy today and start creating jokes that will have the whole family laughing out loud!"

"Copyright © 2023 by Angelo White
All rights reserved.
No part of this book may be reproduced in any form or by any electronic or mechanical means, including information storage and retrieval systems, without permission in writing from the publisher, except by a reviewer who may quote brief passages in a review.
This book is a work of fiction. Names, characters, places, and incidents either are the product of the author's imagination or are used fictitiously. Any resemblance to actual persons, events, or locales is entirely coincidental.

First Edition: 2023
Published by [Angelo White]
Printed in [USA]

"Jokes for Kids is a collection of jokes, riddles, and puns that are specifically tailored for children.

The book is written by Angelo White, a comedian and a father, who shares his expertise on how to create jokes that are both funny and appropriate for children.

The jokes in this book cover a wide range of topics, from puns and wordplay to silly situations and characters. Each joke is presented in a clear and easy-to-understand format, making it easy for children to read and understand.

One of the unique features of this book is that it includes interactive exercises and prompts to help readers come up with their own jokes. This is a great way for children to learn how to create their own jokes and develop their creativity.

Jokes for Kids is not only a great way to entertain children, but it also helps to encourage reading, learning new words, and improving vocabulary, creativity, and imagination. It is suitable for children of all ages and can be enjoyed by the whole family.

Whether you're a parent looking for a fun way to entertain your kids, a teacher looking for a new classroom activity, or just looking for a good laugh, Jokes for Kids is the perfect guide.

With Angelo's clever humor and his wealth of experience, you'll be crafting jokes that will have kids (and adults) laughing in no time. Order your copy today and let the giggles begin!"

Let the giggles begin!

ANGELO WHITE

What does Jeff Bezos do before he goes to sleep?

HE PUTS HIS PJ-AMAZON!

What happened when the world's tongue-twister champion got arrested?

THEY GAVE HIM A TOUGH SENTENCE!

What did the mama cow say to the calf?

IT'S PASTURE BEDTIME!

How does a vampire start a letter?

TOMB IT MAY CONCERN!

What do you call an illegally parked frog?

TOAD!

What did one plate say to the other?

DINNER IS ON ME!

Why do hummingbirds hum?

BECAUSE THEY DON'T KNOW THE WORDS!

What do sprinters eat before a race?

NOTHING. THEY FAST!

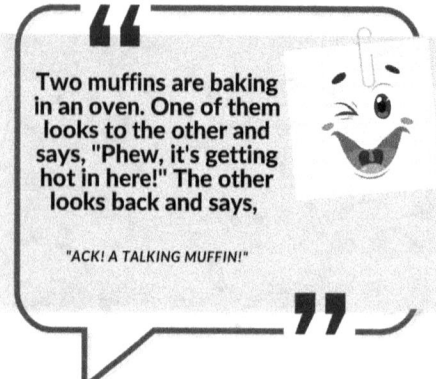

Two muffins are baking in an oven. One of them looks to the other and says, "Phew, it's getting hot in here!" The other looks back and says,

"ACK! A TALKING MUFFIN!"

What do cats eat for breakfast?

MICE CRISPIES!

What do you call an elephant that doesn't matter?

AN IRRELEPHANT!

What do you get when you cross a rabbit with shellfish?

AN OYSTER BUNNY!

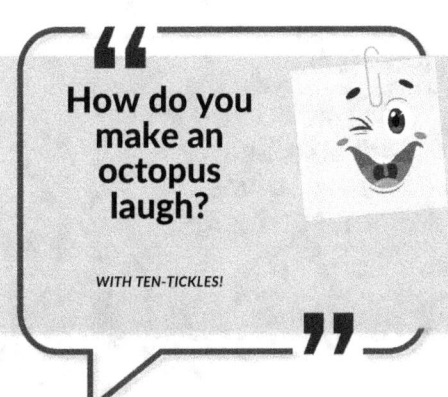

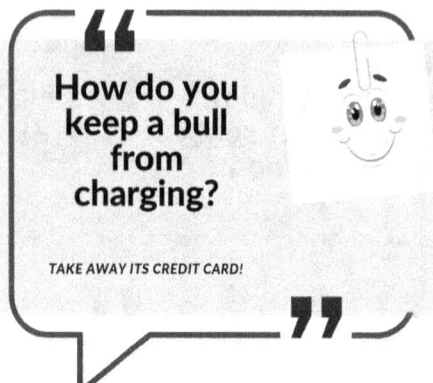

Why is a snake difficult to fool? You can't pull its leg!

NONE, THEY HAVE BEAR FEET!

What do you get when you cross a snail with a porcupine?

A SLOWPOKE!

What did the dog say when it sat on sandpaper?

"RUFF!"

What's a cat's favorite dessert?

CHOCOLATE MOUSE!

What fish only swims at night?

STARFISH!

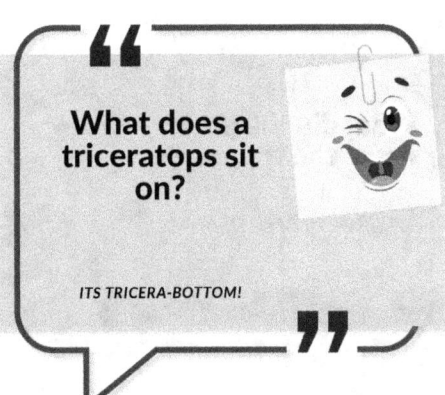

What does a triceratops sit on?

ITS TRICERA-BOTTOM!

What's a piece of bread's least favorite chore?

DOING A LOAF OF LAUNDRY.

What did the bunny say to the carrot?

IT'S BEEN NICE GNAWING YOU!

What do you call a sad strawberry?

BLUEBERRY

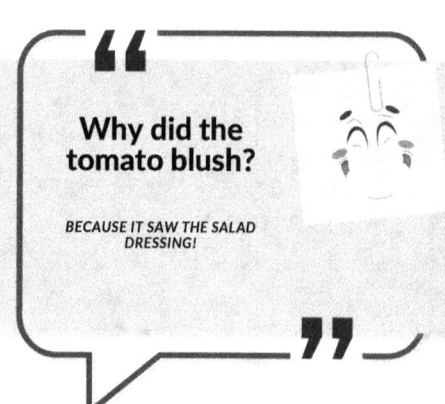

Why did the tomato blush?

BECAUSE IT SAW THE SALAD DRESSING!

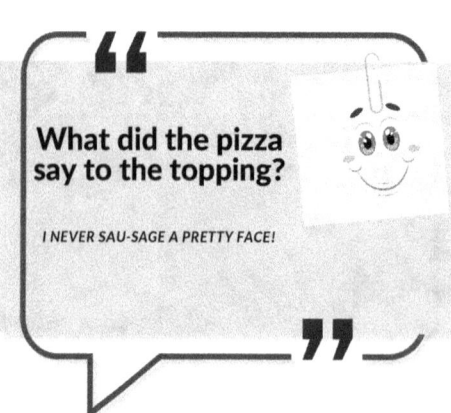

What did the pizza say to the topping?

I NEVER SAU-SAGE A PRETTY FACE!

Which vegetable do sailors hate the most?

LEEKS!

Where does fruit go on vacation?

PEAR-IS!

Why did the melons choose not to get married?

BECAUSE THEY CANTALOUPE!

What does a lemon say when it answers the phone?

YELLOW!

What did one dried fruit say when another asked it to the movies?

IT'S A DATE!

Why do bees have sticky hair?

THEY USE HONEYCOMBS!

What does a cow call an earthquake?

A MILKSHAKE!

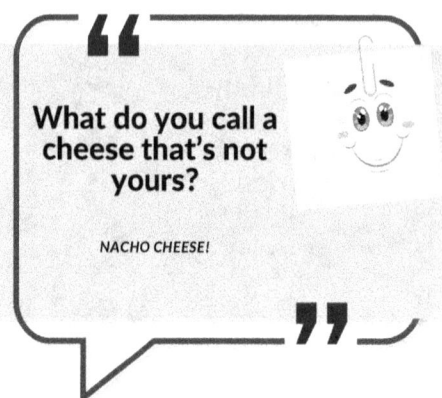

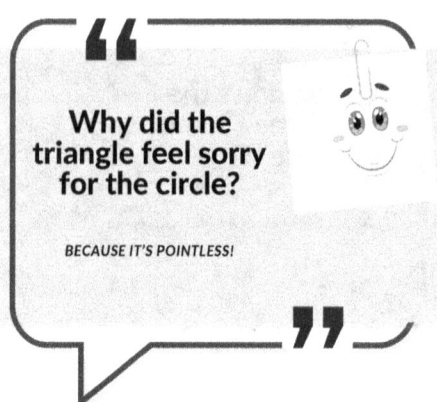

What do you call two guys who love math?

ALGEBROS!

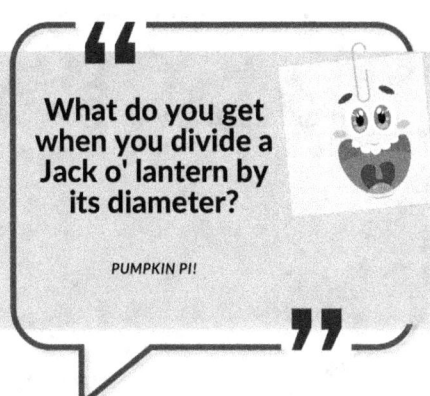

What do you get when you divide a Jack o' lantern by its diameter?

PUMPKIN PI!

What did the 90° angle say after an argument?

"IT TURNS OUT, I WAS RIGHT!"

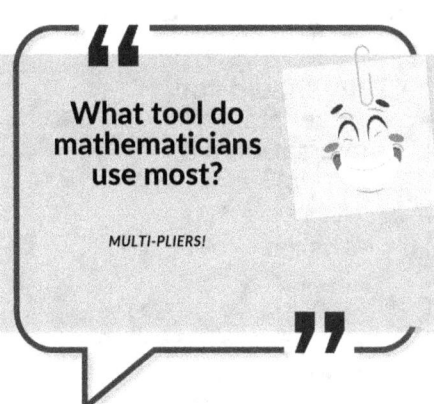

What tool do mathematicians use most?

MULTI-PLIERS!

Why did the student get upset when their teacher called them average?

IT WAS A MEAN THING TO SAY!

If a math teacher had four apples in one hand and five apples in the other hand, what would they have altogether?

REALLY BIG HANDS!

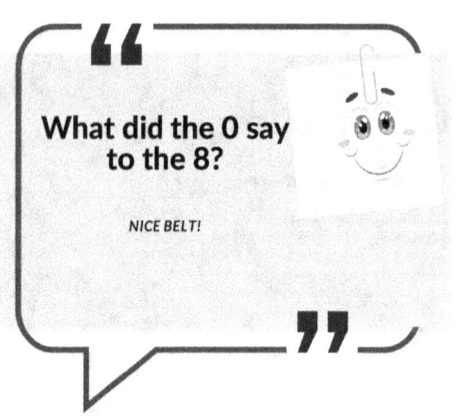

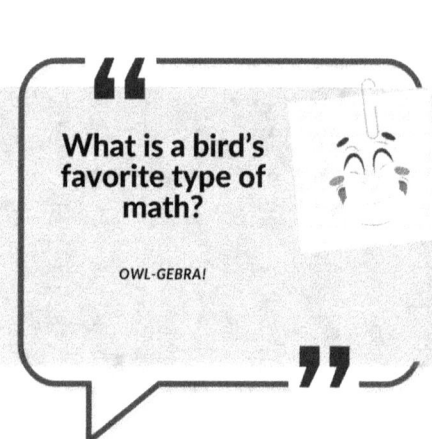

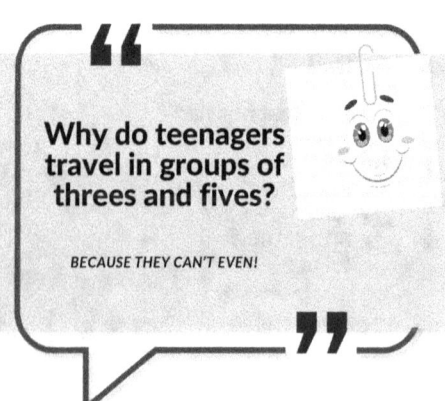

Why are spiders so smart?

THEY CAN FIND EVERYTHING ON THE WEB!

What are mummies' favorite lunches?

WRAPS!

How does Darth Vader like his toast?

ON THE DARK SIDE!

Why are mountains so funny?

THEY'RE JUST HILL AREAS!

Why did the student eat his homework?

BECAUSE HIS TEACHER TOLD HIM IT WOULD BE A PIECE OF CAKE!

What is the Easter bunny's favorite type of music?

HIP-HOP!

What does a book do to keep warm in the winter?

IT PUTS ON A JACKET!

What did the lightbulb say to its sweetheart?

I WUV YOU A WATT!

What's the difference between a guitar and a fish?

YOU CAN TUNE A GUITAR, BUT YOU CAN'T TUNA FISH!

What did the fisherman say to the magician?

PICK A COD, ANY COD!

Why did the picture go to prison?

BECAUSE IT WAS FRAMED!

Why do bicycles fall over?

BECAUSE THEY'RE TWO-TIRED!

> **If a seagull flies over the sea, what flies over the bay?**
>
> A BAGEL!

> **What does the ocean do when it sees its friends?**
>
> IT WAVES!

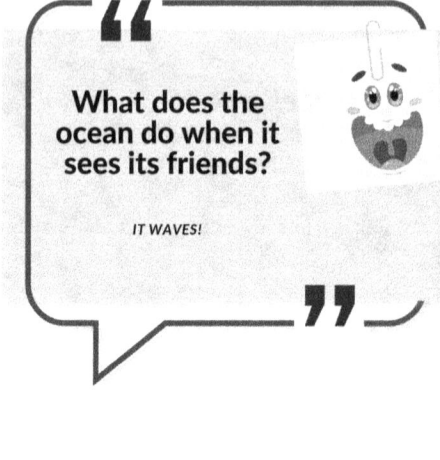

> **Why did the golfer wear two pairs of pants?**
>
> JUST IN CASE HE GOT A HOLE IN ONE!

> **Why do bicycles fallWhy was the broom late? over?**
>
> IT OVER-SWEPT!

> **What did the paper say to the pencil?**
>
> WRITE ON!

> **What do you call a belt made of watches?**
>
> A WAIST OF TIME!

Where do sailboats go when they're sick?

TO THE DOCK!

How does the moon cut his hair?

ECLIPSE IT!

What do you do when a lemon gets sick?

YOU GIVE IT LEMON-AID!

What's worse than raining cats and dogs?

HAILING TAXIS!

How can you tell if a tree is a dogwood tree?

BY ITS BARK!

What do astronauts do before throwing a party?

THEY PLANET!

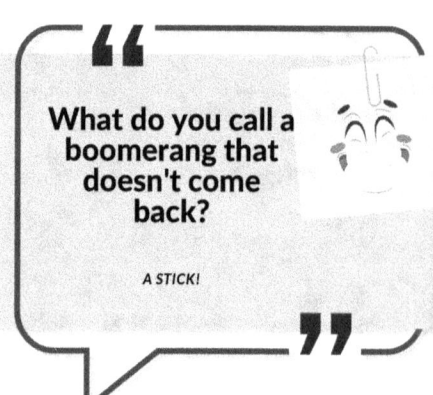
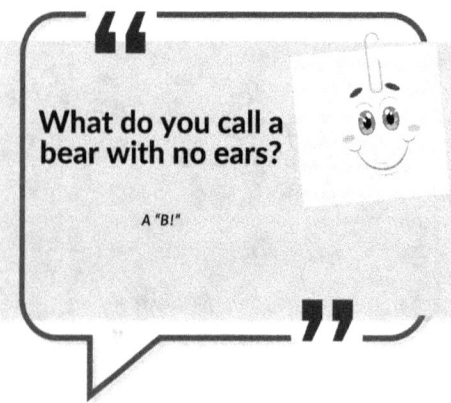

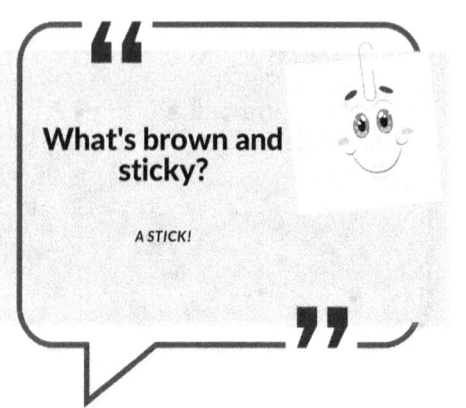
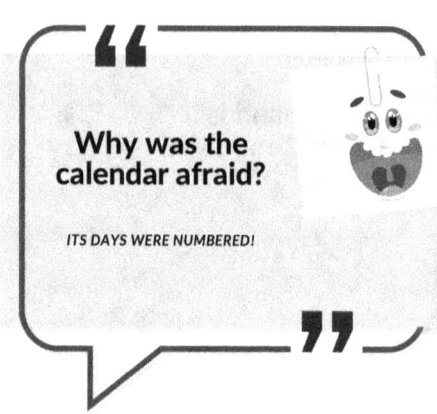

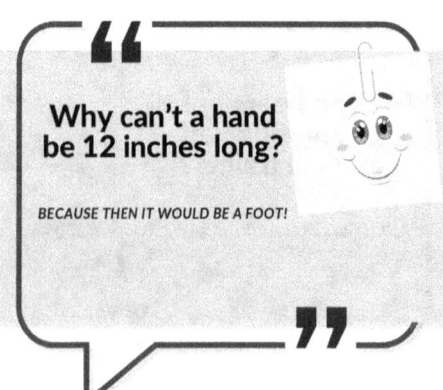

Why are fish so smart?

BECAUSE THEY LIVE IN SCHOOLS!

What did the big flower say to the little flower?

HI, BUD!

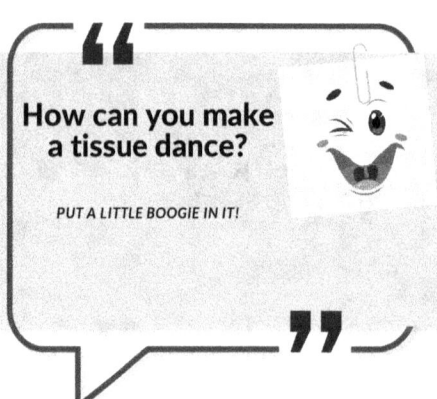

How can you make a tissue dance?

PUT A LITTLE BOOGIE IN IT!

What did the buffalo say when his little boy left for school?

BISON!

What animal can you always find at a baseball game?

A BAT!

Why did the boy throw a stick of butter out the window?

BECAUSE HE WANTED TO SEE A BUTTERFLY!

What did Baby Corn say to Mama Corn?

"WHERE IS POP CORN?"

What do you call a train with a cold?

A-CHOO CHOO TRAIN!

Where do elephants pack their clothes?

IN THEIR TRUNKS!

What do you call a fly without wings?

A WALK!

What do you call a duck that gets straight-As?

A WISE QUACKER!

Why do giraffes have such long necks?

BECAUSE THEY HAVE SMELLY FEET!

> **What did the cop say to their tummy?**
>
> YOU'RE UNDER A VEST!

> **Why did the teddy bear not ask for dessert?**
>
> BECAUSE HE WAS ALREADY SO STUFFED!

> **Which bird is always out of breath?**
>
> A PUFFIN!

> **What's a witch's favorite school subject?**
>
> SPELLING!

> **How do you talk to a giant?**
>
> USE BIG WORDS!

> **Where do sheep go to get their hair cut?**
>
> THE BAA-BAA SHOP!

What do you call a dinosaur that wears glasses?

TYRANNOSAURUS SPECS

What do you call a line of rabbits jumping backwards?

A RECEDING HARE-LINE!

What has four wheels and flies?

A GARBAGE TRUCK!

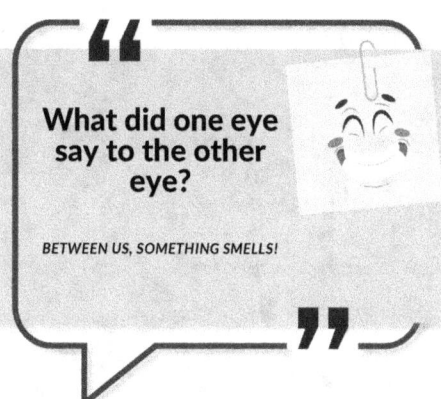

What did one eye say to the other eye?

BETWEEN US, SOMETHING SMELLS!

What did the sink say to the toilet?

WOW, YOU LOOK REALLY FLUSHED!

What gets wetter the more that it dries?

A TOWEL!

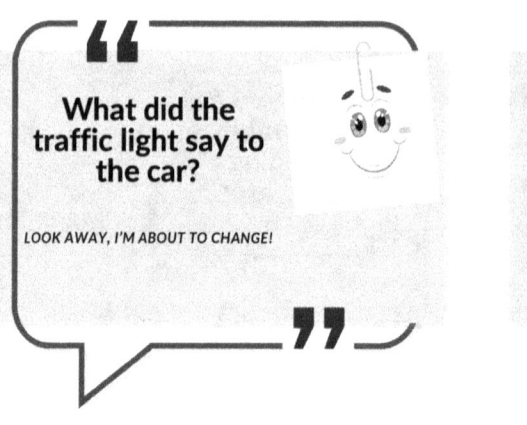

What did the traffic light say to the car?

LOOK AWAY, I'M ABOUT TO CHANGE!

What can you catch, but never throw?

A COLD!

What has more letters than the alphabet?

THE POST OFFICE!

What's black and white and read all over?

A NEWSPAPER!

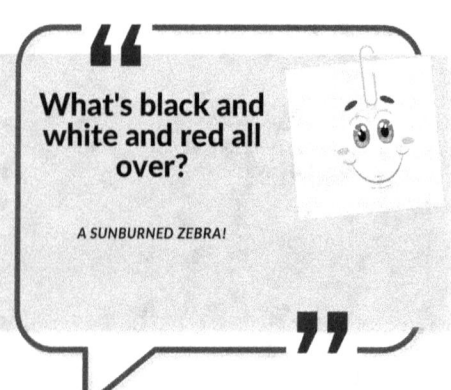

What's black and white and red all over?

A SUNBURNED ZEBRA!

What runs around a baseball field but never moves?

A FENCE!

What is brown and hairy and wears sunglasses?

A COCONUT ON VACATION!

What time is it when an elephant sits on your fence?

TIME TO GET A NEW FENCE!

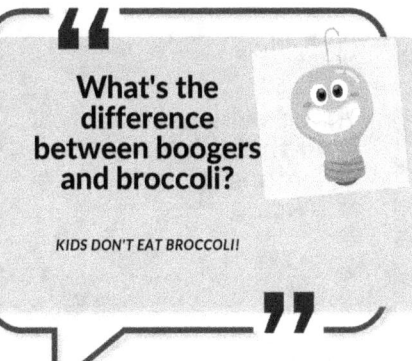

What's the difference between boogers and broccoli?

KIDS DON'T EAT BROCCOLI!

What did the apple say to the worm?

NOTHING, APPLES CAN'T TALK!

What musical instrument can you find in the bathroom?

A TUBA TOOTHPASTE!

What do you call a dinosaur with bad vision?

A DO-YOU-THINK-HE-SARUS!

> **What do you get when you cross a centipede with a parrot?**
>
> A WALKIE TALKIE!

> **Which dinosaur has the best vocabulary?**
>
> THE THESAURUS!

> **Why don't cats like online shopping?**
>
> THEY PREFER A CAT-ALOGUE.

> **What do you call a tiger that drinks lemonade?**
>
> A SOUR PUSS.

> **What do you call a cow with no legs?**
>
> GROUND BEEF.

> **What is a cat's favorite song?**
>
> THREE BLIND MICE.

How do you get a squirrel's attention?

ACT LIKE A NUT.

What do you call birds falling in love?

TWEET HEARTS.

What do you write in a rabbit's birthday card?

HOPPY BIRTHDAY!

What do you call a cold dog?

A CHILI DOG.

What do you call a lazy baby kangaroo?

A POUCH POTATO.

What did the birds call the owl telling jokes?

HOOT-LARIOUS.

> **Why is it so hard for a leopard to hide?**
>
> BECAUSE IT'S ALWAYS SPOTTED.

> **What do you get if you cross a Beatle and an Australian dog?**
>
> DINGO STARR.

> **How do ducks celebrate 4th of July?**
>
> FIREQUACKERS.

> **What do you call an alligator wearing a vest?**
>
> AN INVESTI-GATOR.

> **What type of snake ate all the desserts?**
>
> A PIE-THON.

> **What do cats eat for breakfast?**
>
> MICE KRISPIES

> **How much money does a skunk have?**
>
> ONE SCENT.

> **How do you tell the difference between a bull and a cow?**
>
> IT'S ONE OR THE UDDER.

> **Why do hummingbirds hum?**
>
> BECAUSE THEY DON'T KNOW THE WORDS.

> **Where do polar bears keep their money?**
>
> IN A SNOW BANK.

> **What it it called when a dinosaur makes a soccer goal?**
>
> A DINO-SCORE.

> **Why did the turkey join a band?**
>
> SO SHE COULD USE HER DRUMSTICKS.

> **What is as big as an elephant but weighs nothing?**
>
> AN ELEPHANT'S SHADOW.

> **What's a frog's favorite game?**
>
> LEAPFROG.

> **Why couldn't the duck stop laughing?**
>
> HE WAS QUACKING UP.

> **Who wears shoes while sleeping?**
>
> A HORSE.

> **Why couldn't the pony sing a song?**
>
> SHE WAS A LITTLE HORSE.

> **How do bees get to school?**
>
> A SCHOOL BUZZ.

> **Where do cows go for fun?**
>
> THE MOO-VIES.

> **What is the name of the horse next door?**
>
> NEIGH-BOR.

> **Why do dogs like cell phones?**
>
> THEY HAVE COLLAR ID.

> **What do clouds wear under their clothes?**
>
> THUNDER-WEAR.

> **What did the volcano say to the other?**
>
> I LAVA YOU.

> **Why are sports stadiums always so cold?**
>
> THEY'RE FILLED WITH FANS.

> **What has ears but cannot hear?**
>
> A CORNFIELD.

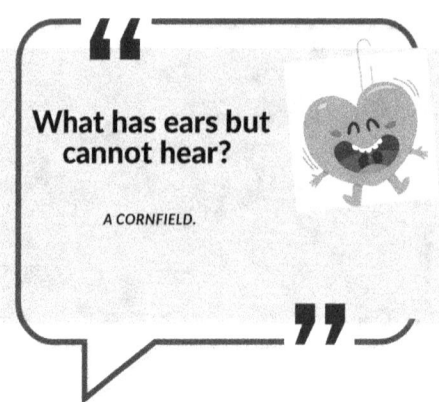

> **What do you call a fake noodle?**
>
> AN IMPASTA.

> **How does a vampire start a letter?**
>
> "TOMB IT MAY CONCERN..."

> **How did the mobile phone propose to his girlfriend?**
>
> HE GAVE HER A RING.

> **What did the right eye say to the left eye?**
>
> BETWEEN US, SOMETHING SMELLS.

> **What do you call a ghost's lover?**
>
> HIS GHOUL-FRIEND.

> **Why can't Elsa have a balloon?**
>
> BECAUSE SHE WILL LET IT GO.

> **What do you cakes and baseball have in common?**
>
> THEY BOTH NEED A BATTER.

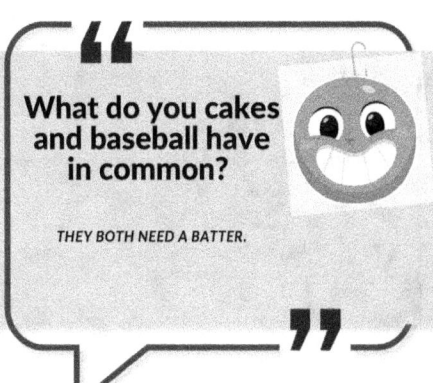

BETWEEN US, SOMETHING SMELLS.

> **What has a head and tail but no body?**
>
> A COIN.

> **Where will you find Friday before Thursday?**
>
> A DICTIONARY.

> **What do elves learn in school?**
>
> THE ELF-ABET.

> **Why was the computer chilly?**
>
> IT LEFT A WINDOW OPEN.

> **How did the cabbage win the race?**
>
> IT WAS A-HEAD.

> **What kind of award did the dentist receive?**
>
> A LITTLE PLAQUE.

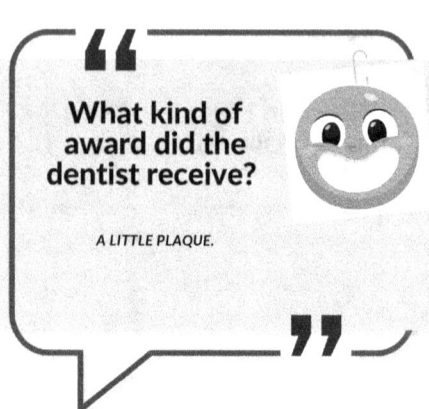

> **What are ten things you can always count on?**
>
> YOUR FINGERS.

> **Why was the equal sign so humble?**
>
> BECAUSE IT WASN'T GREATER THAN OR LESS THAN ANYONE ELSE.

> **What did the triangle say to the circle?**
>
> YOU'RE POINTLESS.

> **What do you get if you divide the circumference of a jack-o-lantern by its diameter?**
>
> PUMPKIN PI.

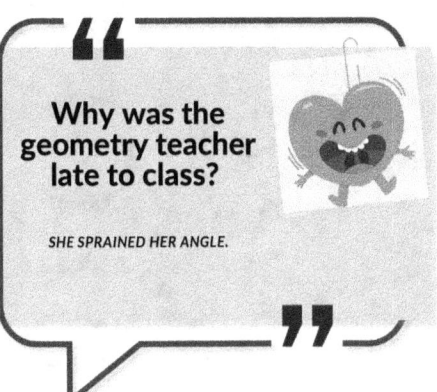

Why was the geometry teacher late to class?

SHE SPRAINED HER ANGLE.

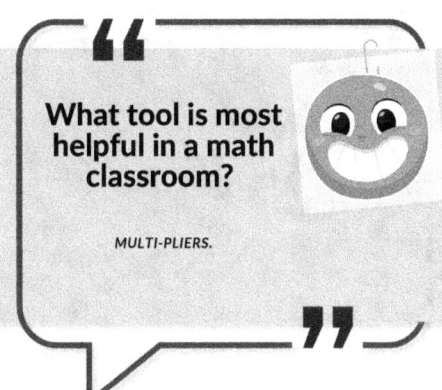

What tool is most helpful in a math classroom?

MULTI-PLIERS.

What's a swimmer's favorite kind of math?

DIVE-ISION.

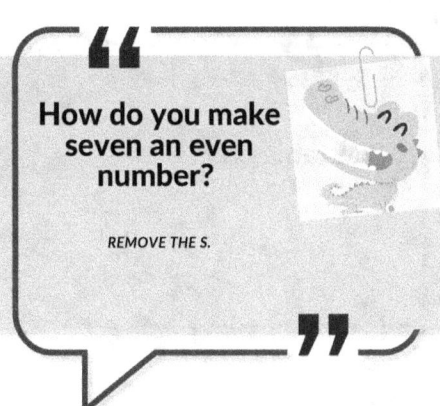

How do you make seven an even number?

REMOVE THE S.

Which king loved fractions?

HENRY THE 8TH.

Why is the obtuse triangle always so irritated?

BECAUSE IT'S NEVER RIGHT.

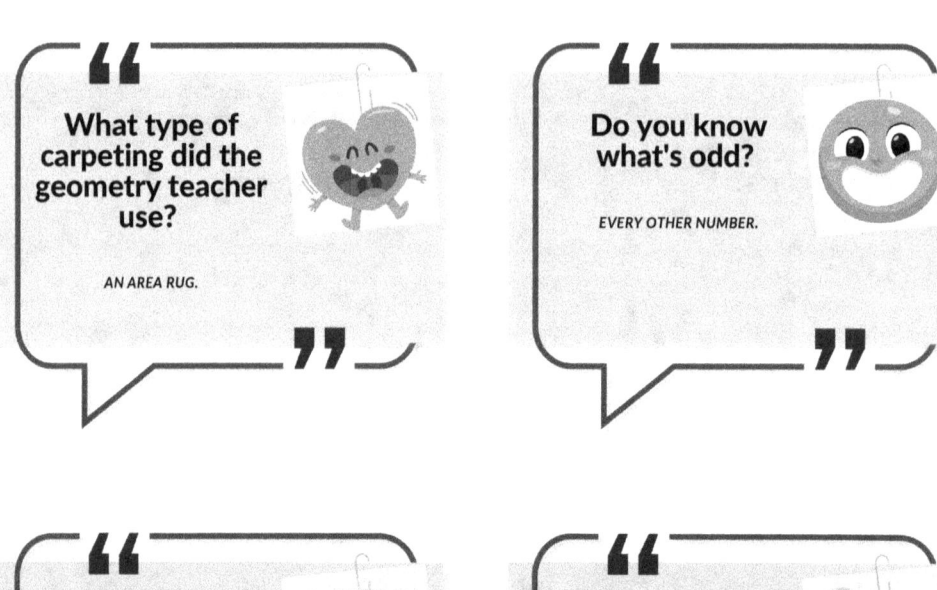

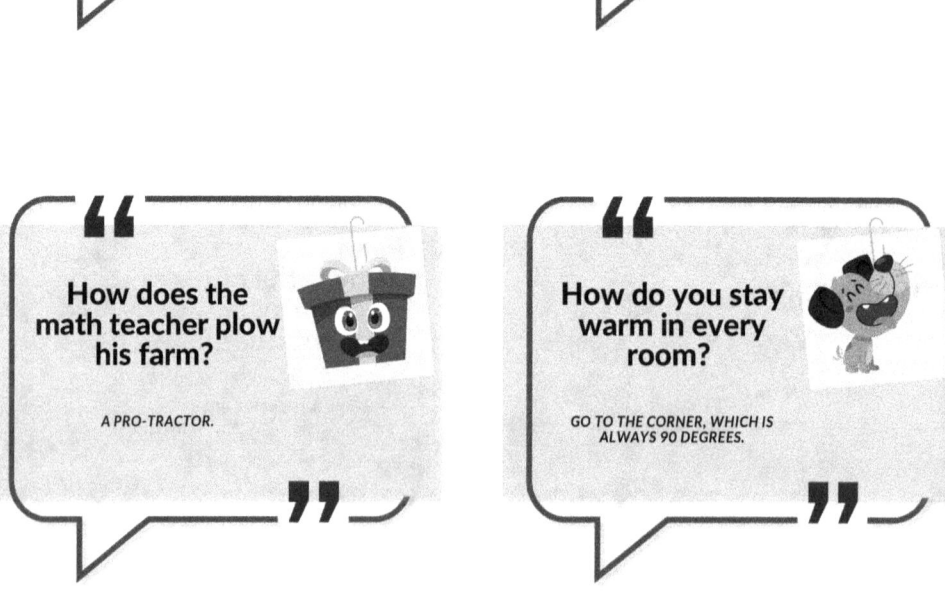

> **Why was the math textbook always so sad?**
>
> IT HAD A TON OF PROBLEMS.

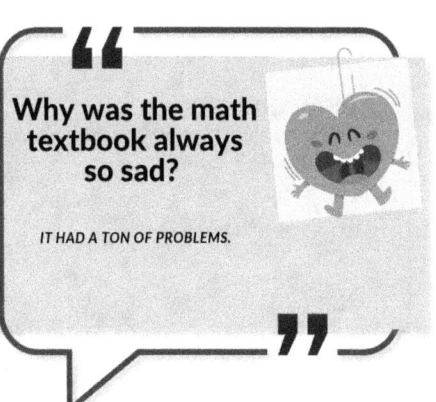

> **If a farmer has 199 sheep, how many will he have when he rounds them up?**
>
> 200.

> **Which knight created the round table?**
>
> SIR CUMFERENCE.

> **What do you get when you milk a cow in Alaska?**
>
> SNOW.

> **What do you call a snowman who goes on vacation in July?**
>
> A PUDDLE.

> **What do snowmen eat for breakfast?**
>
> FROSTED FLAKES.

> **What do you call a snowman on rollerblades?**
>
> A SNOWMOBILE.

> **How do polar bears make their beds?**
>
> SHEETS OF ICE AND BLANKETS OF SNOW.

> **What do snowmen call their kids?**
>
> CHILL-DREN.

> **Why don't mountains get cold in the winter?**
>
> THEY HAVE SNOW CAPS.

> **What kind of ball doesn't bounce?**
>
> A SNOWBALL.

> **What is the best way to decorate a snowman's birthday cake?**
>
> LOTS OF ICE-ING.

> **What is the best way to decorate a snowman's birthday cake?**
>
> LOTS OF ICE-ING.

> **What do you call a snowman's dog?**
>
> SLUSH PUPPY.

> **What do you call a rabbit with fleas?**
>
> BUGS BUNNY.

> **What did one strawberry say to the other strawberry?**
>
> IF YOU WEREN'T SO FRESH, WE WOULDN'T BE IN THIS JAM.

> **When do monkeys fall from the sky?**
>
> APE-RIL SHOWERS.

> **What can fall but never gets hurt?**
>
> RAIN.

What do you call a well-dressed cat?

A DANDY LION.

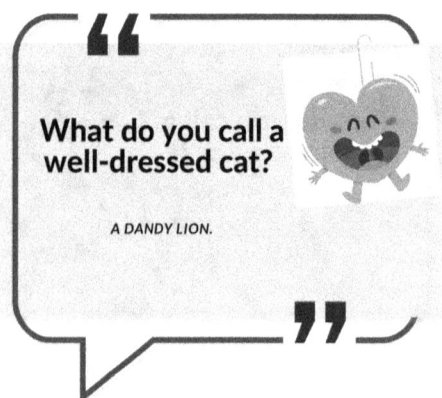

Why did the farmer plant $100 bills?

TO MAKE HIS SOIL RICH.

How do bees brush their hair?

HONEYCOMBS.

Why are the trees so forgiving?

EVERY FALL THEY SAY "LET IT GO."

What kind of bow can't be tied?

A RAINBOW.

What's a chick's favorite food?

EGG-PLANT.

> **What did the pig say on a hot day?**
>
> I'M BACON.

> **Where do sheep spend their summer vacation?**
>
> THE BAAAAA-HAMAS.

> **What do you get when you combine an elephant with a fish?**
>
> SWIMMING TRUNKS.

> **Why don't oysters share their pearls?**
>
> THEY'RE SHELLFISH.

> **Why can't you blame a dolphin for doing something wrong?**
>
> THEY DIDN'T DO IN ON PORPOISE.

> **What type of music do whales listen to?**
>
> ORCA-STRA.

> **Why did the robot take a summer vacation?**
>
> HE NEEDED TO RECHARGE.

> **Why does a seagull fly over the sea?**
>
> BECAUSE IF IT FLEW OVER THE BAY, IT WOULD BE A BAYGULL.

> **What do cats like to eat in the summer?**
>
> MICE CREAM CONES.

> **What is a frog's favorite summertime treat?**
>
> HOPSICLES.

> **What do you call pumpkin who works at the beach?**
>
> A LIFE-GOURD.

> **Which is the cutest of all the seasons?**
>
> AWWW-TUMN.

Who won the skeleton contest?

NO BODY.

Why is Dracula so easy to trick?

HE'S A SUCKER.

What do you get when you drop a pumpkin?

SQUASH.

Why was the jack-o-lantern so afraid?

HE HAD NO GUTS.

Why did the tree fail their exam?

THEY GOT STUMPED ON EVERY QUESTION.

How do trees get on the internet?

THEY LOG ON.

How do you fix a broken pumpkin?

A PUMPKIN PATCH.

What did the sick pumpkin say?

I DON'T FEEL SO GOURD.

What do you call a fish that wears a tie?

A FORMAL TUNA!

Why do cows wear bells?

BECAUSE THEIR HORNS DON'T WORK!

What do you call an alligator in a vest?

AN INVESTIGATOR!

How do you organize a space party?

YOU PLANET!

Why don't scientists trust atoms?

BECAUSE THEY MAKE UP EVERYTHING!

What do you call a bear with no teeth?

A GUMMY BEAR!

What do you call a snake that works for the government?

A CIVIL SERPENT!

Why did the banana go to the doctor?

BECAUSE IT WASN'T PEELING WELL!

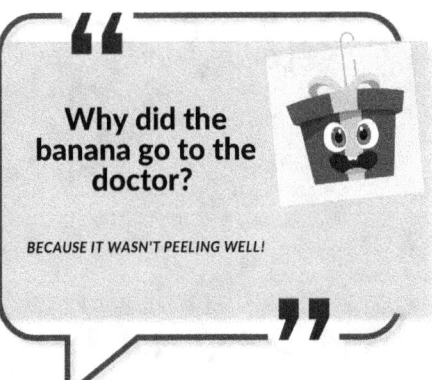

Why did the banana go to the doctor?

BECAUSE IT WASN'T PEELING WELL!

Why did the cookie go to the doctor?

BECAUSE IT WAS FEELING CRUMBLY!

> **What do you call a dinosaur with an extensive vocabulary?**
>
> A THESAURUS!

> **How do you catch a squirrel?**
>
> CLIMB UP IN A TREE AND ACT LIKE A NUT!

> **What do you call a pile of cats?**
>
> A MEOWTAIN!

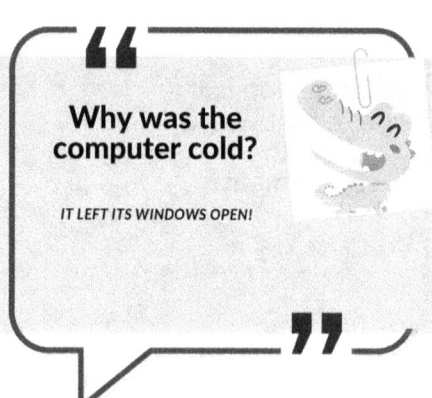

> **Why was the computer cold?**
>
> IT LEFT ITS WINDOWS OPEN!

> **Climb up in a tree and act like a banana!**
>
> CLIMB UP IN A TREE AND ACT LIKE A BANANA!

> **What do you call a sleeping bull?**
>
> A BULLDOZER!

Why do elephants never use computers?

THEY'RE AFRAID OF THE MOUSE!

Why was the belt sent to jail?

IT HELD UP A PAIR OF PANTS!

Why did the golfer bring two pairs of pants?

IN CASE HE GOT A HOLE IN ONE!

Why do cows wear bells?

BECAUSE THEIR HORNS DON'T WORK!

How can a clam cram in a clean cream can?

SHE SELLS SEA SHELLS BY THE SEA SHORE.

What does a cloud wear under his raincoat?

THUNDERWEAR.

> **Two pickles fell out of a jar onto the floor. What did one say to the other?**
> DILL WITH IT.

> **What time is it when the clock strikes 13?**
> TIME TO GET A NEW CLOCK.

> **How does a cucumber become a pickle?**
> IT GOES THROUGH A JARRING EXPERIENCE.

> **What did one toilet say to the other?**
> YOU LOOK A BIT FLUSHED.

> **What do you think of that new diner on the moon?**
> FOOD WAS GOOD, BUT THERE REALLY WASN'T MUCH ATMOSPHERE.

> **Why did the dinosaur cross the road?**
> BECAUSE THE CHICKEN WASN'T BORN YET.

Why did the dinosaur cross the road?

BECAUSE THE CHICKEN WASN'T BORN YET.

How does a scientist freshen her breath?

WITH EXPERI-MINTS.

How are false teeth like stars?

THEY COME OUT AT NIGHT.

What building in your town has the most stories?

THE PUBLIC LIBRARY.

What's worse than finding a worm in your apple?

FINDING HALF A WORM.

What is a computer's favorite snack?

COMPUTER CHIPS.

> **How does the moon cut his hair?**
>
> ECLIPSE IT.

> **How do you talk to a giant?**
>
> USE BIG WORDS.

> **What falls in winter but never gets hurt?**
>
> SNOW.

> **What did the Dalmatian say after lunch?**
>
> THAT HIT THE SPOT.

> **Why did the kid cross the playground?**
>
> TO GET TO THE OTHER SLIDE.

> **What do you call a droid that takes the long way around?**
>
> R2 DETOUR.

> **Why was the baby strawberry crying?**
>
> BECAUSE HER MOM AND DAD WERE IN A JAM.

> **How do you make a lemon drop?**
>
> JUST LET IT FALL.

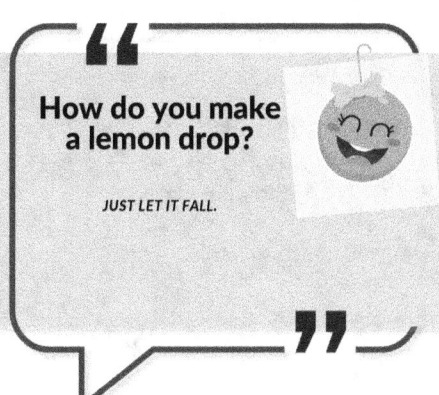

> **What did the limestone say to the geologist?**
>
> DON'T TAKE ME FOR GRANITE.

> **What kind of tree fits in your hand?**
>
> A PALM TREE.

> **What do you call a dinosaur that is sleeping?**
>
> A DINO-SNORE.

> **What is fast, loud and crunchy?**
>
> A ROCKET CHIP.

> **Why did the teddy bear say no to dessert?**
>
> BECAUSE SHE WAS STUFFED.

> **Why do candles always go on the top of cakes?**
>
> BECAUSE IT'S HARD TO LIGHT THEM FROM THE BOTTOM.

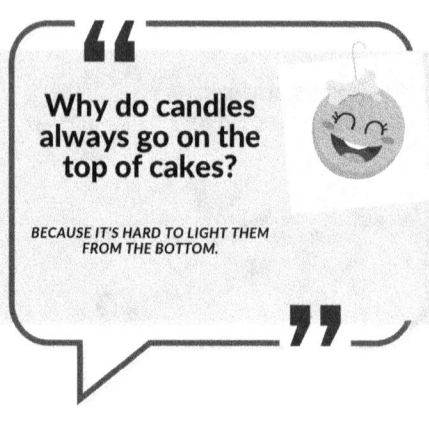

> **What do cakes and baseball teams have in common?**
>
> THEY BOTH NEED A GOOD BATTER.

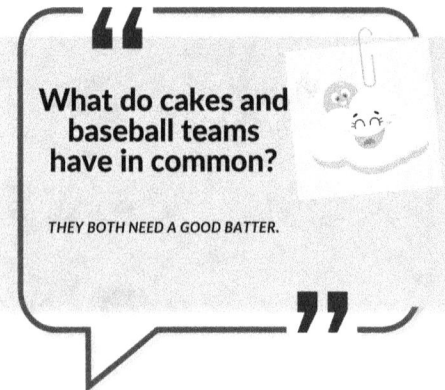

> **What goes up but never comes down?**
>
> YOUR AGE.

> **What does every birthday end with?**
>
> THE LETTER Y.

> **What did the tiger say to her cub on his birthday?**
>
> IT'S ROAR BIRTHDAY.

Why did the girl put her cake in the freezer?

SHE WANTED TO ICE IT.

Does a green candle burn longer than a pink one?

NO, THEY BOTH BURN SHORTER.

Why did the little girl hit her birthday cake with a hammer?

IT WAS A POUND CAKE.

Why did the little girl hit her birthday cake with a hammer?

IT WAS A POUND CAKE.

Are monsters good at math?

NOT UNLESS YOU COUNT DRACULA.

Why does nobody talk to circles?

BECAUSE THERE'S NO POINT.

What was the first animal in space?

THE COW THAT JUMPED OVER THE MOON.

Why don't elephants chew gum?

THEY DO, JUST NOT IN PUBLIC.

What did the banana say to the dog?

BANANAS CAN'T TALK.

How do you make an octopus laugh?

WITH TEN-TICKLES.

How do you fit more pigs on a farm?

BUILD A STY-SCRAPER.

What did the farmer call the cow that had no milk?

AN UDDER FAILURE.

> **What do you call a cow that won't give milk?**
>
> A MILK DUD.

> **What do you get from a pampered cow?**
>
> SPOILED MILK.

> **Where do polar bears vote?**
>
> THE NORTH POLL

> **What sound do porcupines make when they kiss?**
>
> OUCH!

> **Why did the snake cross the road?**
>
> TO GET TO THE OTHER SSSIDE.

> **What did the ocean say to the pirate?**
>
> NOTHING, IT JUST WAVED.

> **Why don't pirates shower before they walk the plank?**
>
> BECAUSE THEY'LL JUST WASH UP ON SHORE LATER.

> **What happened when Bluebeard fell overboard in the Red Sea?**
>
> HE GOT MAROONED.

> **How did the pirate get his flag so cheaply?**
>
> HE BOUGHT IT ON SAIL.

> **What has 8 legs, 8 arms, and 8 eyes?**
>
> 8 PIRATES.

> **How much does it cost a pirate to get his ears pierced?**
>
> ABOUT A BUCK AN EAR.

> **Why is pirating so addictive?**
>
> THEY SAY ONCE YE LOSE YER FIRST HAND, YE GET HOOKED.

> **How do pirates know that they are pirates?**
>
> THEY THINK, THEREFORE THEY ARRR.

> **How do pirates know that they are pirates?**
>
> PURRR-PLE.

> **Where did the school kittens go for their field trip?**
>
> TO THE MEW-SEUM.

> **What kind of kitten works for the Red Cross?**
>
> A FIRST-AID KIT.

> **Why are cats good at video games?**
>
> BECAUSE THEY HAVE NINE LIVES.

> **What did the cat say when he fell off the table?**
>
> "ME-OW."

> **What is the difference between a cat that got photocopied and a cat that follows you?**
>
> ONE IS A CAT COPY; THE OTHER IS A COPY CAT.

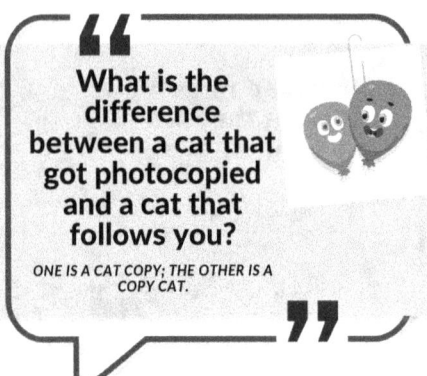

> **What do you get when you cross a ball and a cat?**
>
> A FUR BALL.

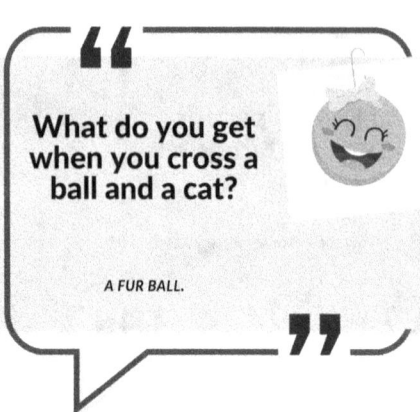

> **Why didn't the skeleton go to school?**
>
> HIS HEART WASN'T IN IT.

> **How does a vampire start a letter?**
>
> TOMB IT MAY CONCERN...

> **What is a monster's favorite dessert?**
>
> I SCREAM.

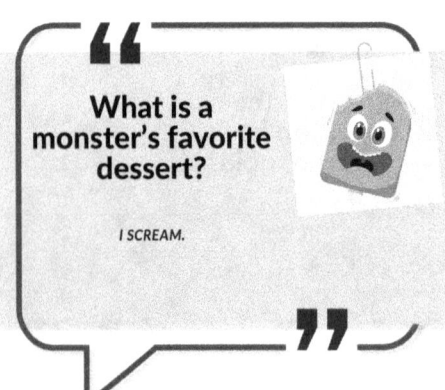

> **What monster plays tricks on Halloween?**
>
> PRANK-ENSTEIN.

> **What kind of music do mummies love?**
>
> WRAP MUSIC.

> **What fruit do scarecrows love the most?**
>
> STRAW-BERRIES.

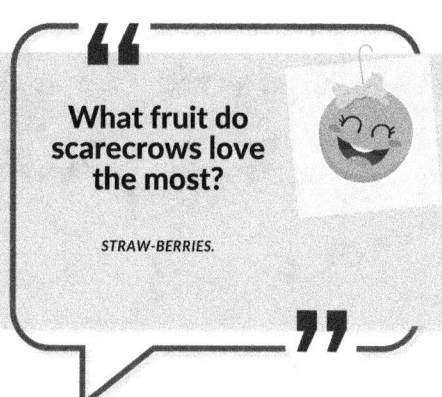

> **What does a witch use to do her hair?**
>
> SCARESPRAY.

> **What room does a ghost not need?**
>
> A LIVING ROOM.

> **What kind of dog does Dracula have?**
>
> A BLOOD HOUND.

> **What is a ghost's nose full of?**
>
> BOO-GERS.

What do birds say on Halloween?

TRICK OR TWEET.

Are black cats bad luck?

SURE, IF YOU'RE A MOUSE.

How do you fix a cracked pumpkin?

A PUMPKIN PATCH.

When is it bad luck to be followed by a black cat?

WHEN YOU'RE A MOUSE.

What do you call two witches living together?

BROOMMATES.

What happens when a vampire goes in the snow?

FROST BITE.

Why did the zombie skip school?

HE WAS FEELING ROTTEN.

What is a vampire's favorite fruit?

A BLOOD ORANGE.

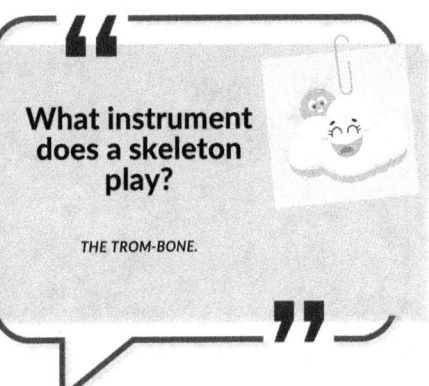

What instrument does a skeleton play?

THE TROM-BONE.

Where do baby ghosts go during the day?

DAY-SCARE CENTERS.

Why didn't the skeleton go to the dance?

BECAUSE HE HAD NO BODY TO GO WITH.

What candy do you eat on the playground?

RECESS PIECES.

> **How do ghosts wash their hair?** 
>
> WITH SHAM-BOO.

> **What's a witch's favorite subject in school?** 
>
> SPELLING.

> **What's big, scary, and has three wheels?** 
>
> A MONSTER ON A TRICYCLE.

> **Why don't vampires have more friends?** 
>
> BECAUSE THEY ARE A PAIN IN THE NECK.

> **What position does a ghost play in hockey?** 
>
> GHOULIE

> **What do you call a witch who goes to the beach?** 
>
> A SAND-WITCH.

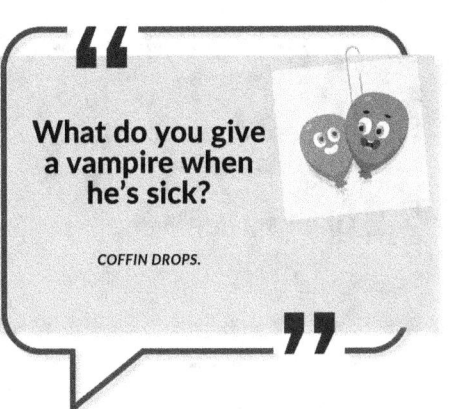

> **What do you give a vampire when he's sick?**
>
> COFFIN DROPS.

> **What kinds of pants do ghosts wear?**
>
> BOO-JEANS.

> **Who isn't hungry at Thanksgiving?**
>
> THE TURKEY—HE'S ALREADY STUFFED.

> **Can a turkey jump higher than Mount Everest?**
>
> YES, BECAUSE A BUILDING CAN'T JUMP AT ALL.

> **Which side of the turkey has the most feathers?**
>
> THE OUTSIDE.

> **What always comes at the end of Thanksgiving?**
>
> THE LETTER G.

> **What's the key to a great Thanksgiving dinner?**
>
> THE TUR-KEY.

> **Where does Christmas come before Thanksgiving?**
>
> IN THE DICTIONARY.

> **Why did pilgrims' pants always fall down?**
>
> BECAUSE THEY WORE THEIR BELT BUCKLE ON THEIR HAT.

> **What do turkeys and teddy bears have in common?**
>
> THEY BOTH HAVE STUFFING.

> **What key won't open any door?**
>
> A TURKEY.

> **Why did the turkey cross the road?**
>
> IT WAS THE CHICKEN'S DAY OFF.

> **Why did the chewing gum cross the road?**
>
> IT WAS STUCK ON THE TURKEY'S FOOT.

> **Why did the turkey cross the road twice?**
>
> TO SHOW HE WASN'T A CHICKEN.

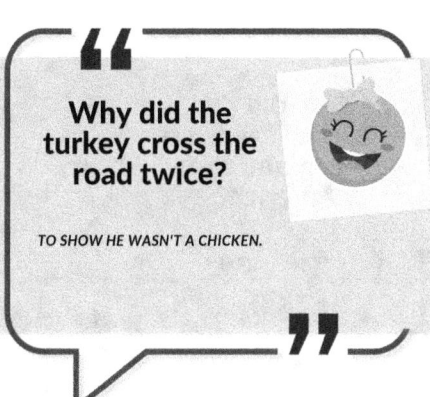

> **What do you get when a turkey lays an egg on top of a barn?**
>
> AN EGGROLL.

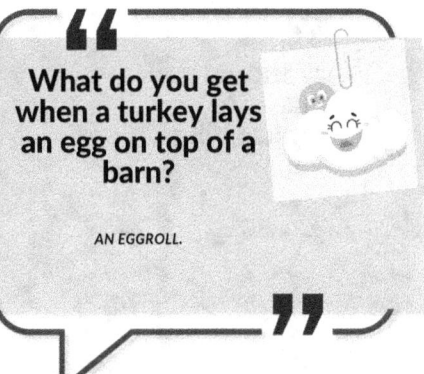

> **Why was the turkey the drummer in the band?**
>
> BECAUSE HE HAD DRUMSTICKS.

> **What's the best thing to put into pumpkin pie?**
>
> YOUR TEETH.

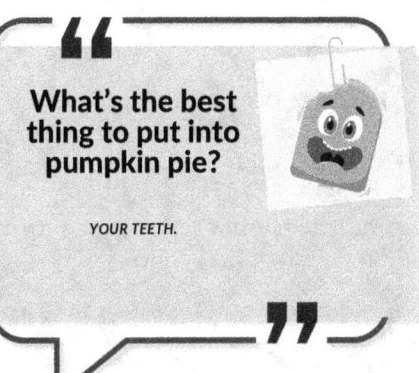

> **What's the best dance to do on Thanksgiving?**
>
> THE TURKEY TROT.

> **Why did the Pilgrims sail from England to America?** 
>
> BECAUSE THEY MISSED THEIR PLANE.

> **When the Pilgrims landed, where did they stand?** 
>
> ON THEIR FEET.

> **Why did the police arrest the turkey?** 
>
> THEY SUSPECTED IT OF FOWL PLAY.

> **What should you wear to Thanksgiving dinner?** 
>
> A HAR-VEST.

> **If the Pilgrims were alive today, what would they be most famous for?** 
>
> THEIR AGE.

> **Where do you find a turkey with no legs?** 
>
> WHERE YOU LEFT IT.

What do you call it when it rains turkeys?

FOUL WEATHER.

Why did the turkey sit on the tomahawk?

TO HATCH-ET.

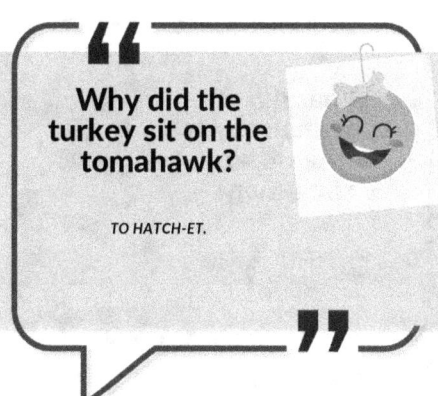

What kind of music did Pilgrims listen to?

PLYMOUTH ROCK.

What smells the best at a Thanksgiving dinner?

YOUR NOSE.

Why do turkeys always say, "gobble, gobble"?

BECAUSE THEY NEVER LEARNED GOOD TABLE MANNERS.

How does a snowman lose weight?

HE WAITS FOR THE WEATHER TO GET WARMER.

> **In what year does New Year's Day come before Christmas?**
>
> EVERY YEAR.

> **What do snowmen eat for breakfast?**
>
> FROSTED FLAKES.

> **What kind of motorcycle does Santa like to ride?**
>
> A HOLLY DAVIDSON.

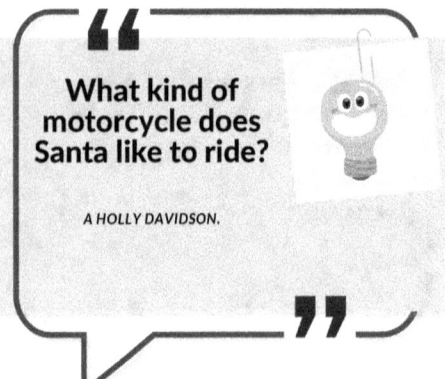

> **Why are Christmas trees bad at sewing?**
>
> BECAUSE THEY ALWAYS DROP THEIR NEEDLES.

> **What do you get when Santa becomes a detective?**
>
> SANTA CLUES.

> **Why was the Easter Bunny so upset?**
>
> HE WAS HAVING A BAD HARE DAY.

How did the soggy Easter Bunny dry himself?

WITH A HARE DRYER.

How does the Easter bunny stay in shape?

LOTS OF EGGS-ERCISE.

Why can't a rabbit's nose be 12 inches long?

BECAUSE THEN IT WOULD BE A FOOT.

How can you tell which rabbits are the oldest in a group?

JUST LOOK FOR THE GRAY HARES.

What do you call a bunny who isn't smart?

A HARE BRAIN.

What's the best way to catch a unique rabbit?

UNIQUE UP ON HIM.

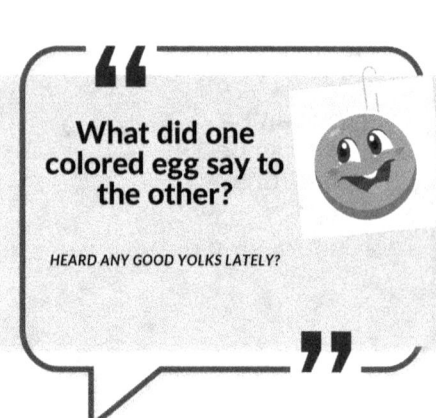

What kind of jewelry do rabbits wear?

14 CARROT GOLD.

How many chocolate bunnies can you put into an empty Easter basket?

ONLY ONE BECAUSE AFTER THAT, IT'S NOT EMPTY.

What do you call a rabbit with fleas?

BUGS BUNNY.

Why did the Easter egg hide?

HE WAS A LITTLE CHICKEN.

Why did the robber jump in the shower?

HE WANTED TO MAKE A CLEAN GETAWAY.

What kind of shoes do robbers wear?

SNEAKERS.

"Knock, knock! Who's there? Says. Says who? Says me!"

"Knock, knock! Who's there? Woo. Woo who? Glad you're excited, too."

"Knock, knock! Who's there? Orange. Orange who? Orange you going to let me in?"

"Knock, knock. Who's there? Needle. Needle who? Needle little help right now!"

"Knock, knock. Who's there? Weekend. Weekend who? Weekend do anything we want!"

"Knock, knock. Who's there? Figs. Figs who? Figs the doorbell, I've been knocking forever!"

Knock, knock.
Who's there?
Theodore.
Theodore who?
Theodore wasn't opened so I knocked!

Knock, knock.
Who's there?
Tank.
Tank who?
You're welcome!

Knock, knock.
Who's there?
Isabel.
Isabel who?
Isabel not working?

Knock, knock.
Who's there?
Ice cream.
Ice cream who?
ICE CREAM SO YOU CAN HEAR ME!

Knock, knock.
Who's there?
Icy.
Icy who?
Icy you in there!

Knock, knock.
Who's there?
Dozen.
Dozen who?
Dozen anyone want to let me in?

"Knock, knock.
Who's there?
Scold.
Scold who?
Scold outside, let me in!"

"Knock, knock.
Who's there?
Water.
Water who?
Water you asking so many questions for, just open up!"

"Knock, knock.
Who's there?
Cargo.
Cargo who?
Car go, "Toot toot, vroom, vroom!""

"Knock, knock.
Who's there?
Hatch.
Hatch who?
Bless you!"

"Knock, knock.
Who's there?
Annie.
Annie who?
Annie body home?"

"Knock, knock.
Who's there?
Boo.
Boo who?
Don't cry, it's just a joke!"

> I scream, you scream, we all scream, for ice cream!

I SCREAM

> Peter Piper picked a peck of pickled peppers
>
> A peck of pickled peppers Peter Piper picked
> If Peter Piper picked a peck of pickled peppers
>
> Where's the peck of pickled peppers that Peter Piper picked?

PETER PIPER

> Betty Botter bought a bit of butter.
>
> "But," she said, "this bit of butter's bitter,
> But a bit of better butter mixed with this butter might just make my bit of bitter butter better."
>
> So, Betty bought a bit of better butter to make her bitter butter better.

BETTY BOTTER

> I saw Susie sitting in a shoe shine shop.
>
> Where she shines, she sits, and where she sits, she shines.

SUSIE SHINE

> How much wood would a woodchuck chuck, if the woodchuck could chuck wood?
>
> He would chuck, he would, as much as he could,
>
> And chuck as much wood as a woodchuck would,
> If a woodchuck could chuck wood.

WOODCHUCK

> If one doctor doctors another doctor, Then which doctor is doctoring the doctored doctor?
>
> Does the doctor who doctors the doctor, doctor the doctor the way the doctor he is doctoring doctors?
>
> Or does he doctor the doctor the way the doctor who doctors doctors?

DOCTOR DOCTOR

> I thought a thought,
> But the thought I thought wasn't the thought I thought I thought.
> If the thought I thought I thought had been the thought I thought,
> I wouldn't have thought so much.
>
> **THOUGHT A THOUGHT**

> Fuzzy Wuzzy was a bear,
> Fuzzy Wuzzy had no hair,
> Fuzzy Wuzzy wasn't very fuzzy, was he?
>
> **FUZZY WUZZY**

> She sells sea shells by the seashore
>
> And the shells she sells by the seashore are sea shells for sure.
>
> **SHE SELLS**

> All I want is a proper cup of coffee,
> Made in a proper copper coffee pot
> I may be off my dot
> But I want a cup of coffee
> From a proper coffee pot.
>
> Tin coffee pots and iron coffee pots
> They're no use to me –
> If I can't have a proper cup of coffee
> In a proper copper coffee pot
> I'll have a cup of tea.
>
> **ALL I WANT IS A PROPER CUP OF COFFEE**

> Brave, bleeding boys battle bald, biting babies
>
> Biting babies ride battle toys while bumbling boys brave bald biting babies.
>
> **BLEEDING BOYS**

> Denise sees the fleece,
> Denise sees the fleas.
>
> At least Denise could sneeze
> And feed and freeze the fleas.
>
> **DENISE SEES**

> To sit in solemn silence in a dull, dark dock,
>
> In a pestilential prison, with a life-long lock,
> Awaiting the sensation of a short, sharp shock,
>
> From a cheap and chippy chopper on a big black block!
>
> **DARK DOCK**

> Luke Luck likes lakes.
> Luke's duck likes lakes.
>
> Luke Luck licks lakes.
> Luke's duck licks lakes.
> Duck takes licks in lakes Luke Luck likes.
>
> Luke Luck takes licks in lakes duck likes.
>
> **LUKE LUCK**

> Through three cheese trees three free fleas flew
>
> While these fleas flew, freezy breeze blew
> Freezy breeze made these three trees freeze
>
> Freezy trees made these trees' cheese freeze
> That's what made these three free fleas sneeze
>
> **CHEESE TREES**

> Black background, brown background,
>
> Brown background, black background,
> Background background, black, black, brown, brown.
>
> **BLACK AND BROWN BACKGROUND**

> Why do you cry, Willy?
> Why, Willy?
> Why, why, why?!
> Why do you cry?
> Willy, Willy!
> Willy cry, why you cry, Willy?
>
> **WHY WILLY?!**

> Ned Nott was shot and Sam Shott was not.
> So it is better to be Shott than Nott.
>
> Some say Nott was not shot.
> But Shott says he shot Nott.
> Either the shot Shott shot at Nott was not shot,
> Or Nott was shot.
>
> If the shot Shott shot shot Nott, Nott was shot.
> But if the shot Shott shot shot Shott,
> Then Shott was shot, not Nott.
>
> However, the shot Shott shot shot not Shott, but Nott.
>
> **NED NOTT AND SAM SHOTT**

> Yellow butter, purple jelly, red jam, black bread.
>
> Spread it thick, say it quick!
> Yellow butter, purple jelly, red jam, black bread.
>
> Spread it thicker, say it quicker!
> Yellow butter, purple jelly, red jam, black bread.
>
> Don't eat until you are spreading it like a spread!
>
> **BUTTER AND JELLY**

> Chester cheetah chews a chunk of cheap cheddar cheese
>
> If the chunk of cheese chunked Chester cheetah,
> What would Chester cheetah chew and chunk on?
>
> **CHESTER CHEETAH**

> What did the policeman say to his belly button?
>
> **YOU'RE UNDER A VEST!**

> Why shouldn't you write with a broken pencil?
>
> **BECAUSE IT'S POINTLESS.**

> What did the judge say when the skunk walked in the court room?
>
> **ODOR IN THE COURT.**

> What did the janitor say when he jumped out of the closet?
>
> **SUPPLIES!!!!!!!**

Why couldn't the pirate play cards?

BECAUSE HE WAS SITTING ON THE DECK!

What did one elevator say to the other elevator?

I THINK I'M COMING DOWN WITH SOMETHING!

Why couldn't the bicycle stand up by itself?

IT WAS TWO-TIRED!

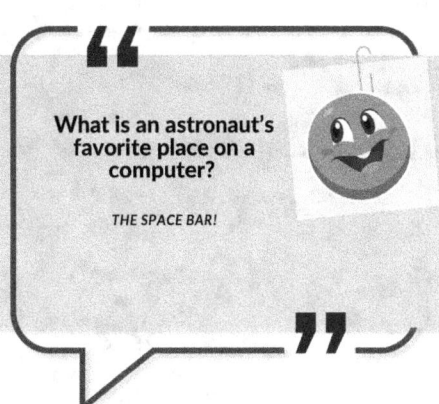

What is an astronaut's favorite place on a computer?

THE SPACE BAR!

Why did the scarecrow win an award?

BECAUSE HE WAS "OUT STANDING" IN HIS FIELD.

What did one hat say to another?

YOU STAY HERE, I'LL GO ON A HEAD

> **How do you make a tissue dance?**
>
> YOU PUT A LITTLE BOOGIE IN IT!

> **Why did the math book need to see a counselor?**
>
> BECAUSE IT WAS FULL OF PROBLEMS!

> **What do you get someone who already has everything?**
>
> A BURGLAR ALARM!

> **Why did the golfer wear two pairs of pants?**
>
> IN CASE HE GOT A HOLE IN ONE!

> **What is more impressive than a talking parrot?**
>
> A SPELLING BEE!

> **Why didn't the Teddy Bear eat dessert?**
>
> BECAUSE HE WAS STUFFED!

Why did the boy bring a ladder to school?

HE WANTED TO GO TO HIGH SCHOOL!

What happened to the frog who's car broke down?

HE HAD TO BE TOAD.

Have you seen the movie "Constipated"?

NO, IT HASN'T COME OUT YET!

What did the traffic light say to the car?

DON'T PEAK, I'M CHANGING!

What goes up and down but does not move?

STAIRS

Where should a 500 pound alien go?

ON A DIET

> **Why did the picture go to jail?**
>
> *BECAUSE IT WAS FRAMED.*

> **What did one wall say to the other wall?**
>
> *I'LL MEET YOU AT THE CORNER.*

> **What do you call a boy named Lee that no one talks to?**
>
> *LONELY*

> **What gets wetter the more it dries?**
>
> *A TOWEL.*

> **Why do dragons sleep during the day?**
>
> *SO THEY CAN FIGHT KNIGHTS!*

> **What did Cinderella say when her photos did not show up?**
>
> *SOMEDAY MY PRINTS WILL COME!*

> Why was the broom late?
>
> IT OVER SWEPT!

> What part of the car is the laziest?
>
> THE WHEELS, BECAUSE THEY ARE ALWAYS TIRED!

> What did the stamp say to the envelope?
>
> STICK WITH ME AND WE WILL GO PLACES!

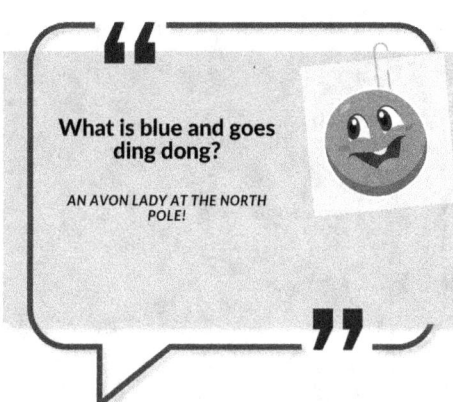

> What is blue and goes ding dong?
>
> AN AVON LADY AT THE NORTH POLE!

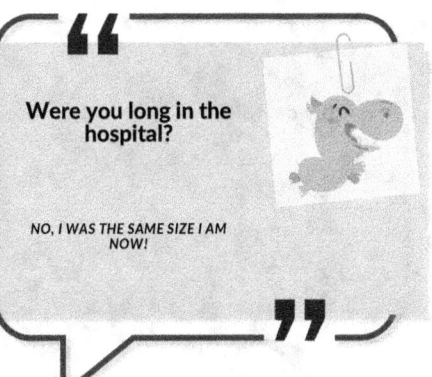

> Were you long in the hospital?
>
> NO, I WAS THE SAME SIZE I AM NOW!

> What did the laundryman say to the impatient customer?
>
> KEEP YOUR SHIRT ON!

"What is green and has yellow wheels?"

GRASS.....I LIED ABOUT THE WHEELS!

"What is it that even the most careful person overlooks?"

HER NOSE!

"Did you hear about the robbery last night?"

TWO CLOTHES PINS HELD UP A PAIR OF PANTS!

"Why do you go to bed every night?"

BECAUSE THE BED WON'T COME TO YOU!

"Why did Billy go out with a prune?"

BECAUSE HE COULDN'T FIND A DATE!

"Why do eskimos do their laundry in Tide?"

BECAUSE IT'S TOO COLD OUT-TIDE!

> **How do you cure a headache?**
>
> PUT YOUR HEAD THROUGH A WINDOW AND THE PANE WILL JUST DISAPPEAR!

> **What has four wheels and flies?**
>
> A GARBAGE TRUCK!

> **Why don't traffic lights ever go swimming?**
>
> BECAUSE THEY TAKE TOO LONG TO CHANGE!

> **Why did the man run around his bed?**
>
> TO CATCH UP ON HIS SLEEP!

> **Why did the man run around his bed?**
>
> TO CATCH UP ON HIS SLEEP!

> **Why did Santa go to music school?**
>
> SO HE COULD IMPROVE HIS WRAPPING SKILLS

> **Why did the man run around his bed?**
>
> TO CATCH UP ON HIS SLEEP.

> **What nails do carpenters hate hammering?**
>
> FINGERNAILS

> **Why did the teacher put on sunglasses?**
>
> BECAUSE HER STUDENTS WERE SO BRIGHT!

> **What do you call a flower that runs on electricity?**
>
> A POWER PLANT!

> **How do you keep a bull from charging?**
>
> TAKE AWAY ITS CREDIT CARD!

> **Why do the French like to eat snails?**
>
> BECAUSE THEY DON'T LIKE FAST FOOD!

Thank you for choosing Jokes for Kids!

We are thrilled that you have decided to join us on this journey of laughter and fun. We hope that this book will bring endless joy and entertainment to you and your family.

We are grateful for your support and we appreciate your trust in us. We promise to continue providing you with the best quality content that will entertain and educate you at the same time.

Don't hesitate to reach out to us if you have any questions or comments about the book. We are always happy to hear from our customers.

Once again, thank you for choosing Jokes for Kids. We wish you and your family many hours of laughter and fun.

Sincerely, Angelo White

www.ingramcontent.com/pod-product-compliance
Lightning Source LLC
Chambersburg PA
CBHW050301120526
44590CB00016B/2448